Joy Makers – Joy Takers

A Five Week Study on the Book of Philippians

by
Cammy Tidwell with Sheryl Vasso

Dedication

This work is dedicated to "the girls" at Child Evangelism Fellowship in Harrisburg, PA – Miss Mable Ruth, Miss Rita and Miss Ginny – you bring us great joy!
and
To the women from Northern India who attended the Women's Conference during the Diamond Jubilee Anniversary of the Hindustan Bible Institute, August 2012 in Chennai, India.

"Those who look to him for help will be radiant with joy; no shadow of shame will darken their faces."
Psalm 34:5 (NLT)

Table of Contents

Introduction

Happiness is Fleeting, but Joy is Forever

*H*appiness is a big deal. It was a big deal to America's founding fathers as they reinforced the pursuit of happiness as an unalienable right of the nation's citizens. Even the cartoon character Charlie Brown made a big deal out of happiness by defining it in song:

HAPPINESS IS FINDING A PENCIL
PIZZA WITH SAUSAGE
TELLING THE TIME
HAPPINESS IS LEARNING TO WHISTLE
TYING YOUR SHOE FOR THE VERY FIRST TIME

HAPPINESS IS PLAYING THE DRUM IN YOUR OWN SCHOOL BAND
HAPPINESS IS WALKING HAND IN HAND
 HAPPINESS IS TWO KINDS OF ICE CREAM
KNOWING A SECRET
CLIMBING A TREE
HAPPINESS IS FIVE DIFFERENT CRAYONS
CATCHING A FIREFLY
SETTING HIM FREE

HAPPINESS IS BEING ALONE EVERY NOW AND THEN
HAPPINESS IS COMING HOME AGAIN
HAPPINESS IS MORNING AND EVENING
DAY TIME AND NIGHT TIME, TOO
FOR HAPPINESS IS ANYONE AND ANYTHING AT ALL
THAT'S LOVED BY YOU

HAPPINESS IS HAVING A SISTER
SHARING A SANDWICH
GETTING ALONG
HAPPINESS IS SINGING TOGETHER WHEN DAY IS THROUGH
AND HAPPINESS IS THOSE WHO SING WITH YOU
HAPPINESS IS MORNING AND EVENING
DAY TIME AND NIGHT TIME, TOO
FOR HAPPINESS IS ANYONE AND ANYTHING AT ALL
THAT'S LOVED BY YOU
(From "You're a Good Man, Charlie Brown")

As much as this is a fun and memorable song, the truth of the lyrics is the happiness the world has to offer is based on circumstances and is often fleeting. What if we can't find a number two pencil, or share a sandwich, or what if we don't have a sister? Do we then become unhappy? The happiness the world has to offer is a fair weather fan at best. As long as the circumstances are favorable, happiness can exist. However, we need to stop listening to the world and start listening to the Word of God.

The Word of God does not mention happiness as much as it does joy. When joy is mentioned, it is always related to God and it is always a permanent possession. It is not a matter of having pizza with sausage, but it is always a matter of something that only true believers in Christ can have. Someone once described joy as the "flag that flies over the castle of the heart when the King is in residence." How do we get this kind of joy? Perhaps the best place to start is with Paul, the apostle and the author of the joy epistle, Philippians!

"Happiness is the level of the soul dependent on outward circumstances (nothing there to ruffle things), whereas joy is a spiritual quality independent of outward circumstances."
-Chuck Smith

Week One

Introduction

Recently I had a conversation with a man who reads the Bible through every year. Now I know many people who do this, but the way he approached this task was fascinating. Every January as he began reading Scripture, he had a different question in mind. One year he read the Bible asking, "What can I learn about being a father?" Another year as he read, he looked for leadership principles he could use in the workplace. At this point, his wife gently teased him that it was "her turn" – meaning it was time he read it through to improve his skill at being a husband.

On a smaller, but similar scale, Sheryl and I recently read an Advent Devotional that was comprised of writings by Dietrich Bonheoffer who was a German pastor, theologian and ultimately a martyr for his stance against the Nazi regime and for the cause of Christ. Most of the entries were written while he was imprisoned during the final years of Hitler's reign of destruction and terror that gripped the entire world. Every day as we read, we found it impossible to remove ourselves from the context of Bonheoffer's words. When he wrote about God being the Lord over fear, we imagined the people of the towns and villages living in a state of panic awaiting the next air raid or bombing. It changed the way we viewed Bonheoffer's writings because we put ourselves into the context of his life circumstances.

Throughout this book, our goal is to approach the book of Philippians with the same mindset. We will read the book and study its principles with a view from Paul's jail cell. Our goal will be twofold:

to keep in mind Paul's circumstances as he wrote and to apply the principles we find to the topic of joy. In every chapter we will identify Joy Takers and seek to overcome them with the more powerful Joy Makers. In this way, this particular study of Philippians is a bit of a hybrid. We will use some inductive study techniques, but our applications will be geared toward finding true and lasting joy and contentment in Christ.

One commentator had this to say about the book of Philippians: "You will find Philippians a beautiful and profitable book which contains many principles of life that will literally transform your attitude toward people and circumstances." Do you need this kind of transformation? Don't you think we all do? At its simplest form, life really is nothing more than a set of people engaged in a series of circumstances and how we choose to act or respond to both. With that in mind, let's get started.

Week One

Day 1

As we begin our study of the book of Philippians, the most important aspect of the time we set aside to focus on God's Word will be beginning each day in prayer. This is a step we may most often be tempted to skip, but it is vital. It doesn't have to be a long prayer filled with formal words – a simple sentence prayer will do. At the beginning of each day of study, we will find one verse from Psalm 119 to use as a springboard as we ask God to open our hearts to what He wants to teach us.

"Open my eyes, that I may behold wonderful things from Your law."
Psalm 119:18

Our first assignment is to simply read through the book of Philippians without stopping to ponder, question or meditate. Rather, we will just sit down and read it as if it were a letter that has just come in the mail. Now, before you get up for that next cup of coffee, read it again slowly. If you can, read it out loud.

Over the next few weeks you will read the book of Philippians numerous times. We have found that in addition to reading the Bible, listening to the passages adds another dimension. There are several ways to do this, but one very convenient way is through an app on your smart phone or computer and many Bible apps are free! It will take approximately 15 minutes to listen to the book of Philippians. You will be amazed at what you absorb differently when you hear the Word of God.

After reading the book a couple of times record your first

impressions and answer the following questions:

What kind of letter is it?

What prompted Paul to write to the Philippians?

Was there any indication how Paul felt about these people?

What is the tone of the letter? Is it encouraging?

Record any other thoughts or questions that come to your mind today. Can you see that studying this book of the Bible can offer you an attitude adjustment?

Write a prayer to God committing yourself to this study and ask Him to help you be willing to change your perspective and point of view in areas of your life where you have lost your joy.

Week One

Day 2

"I will meditate on Your precepts and regard Your ways."
Psalm 119:15

When we open in prayer today, let's ask God to give us a heart to meditate on His ways and to open our hearts to His precepts as we study the book of Philippians.

Today's assignment is twofold: find out as much as you can about Paul and then do the same for the recipients of his letter, the church at Philippi. To learn about Paul from the book of Philippians, we must read the text with the intention of noticing everything Paul says about himself. Read through all four chapters and mark every reference to Paul.

Where was Paul at the time of this writing?

Are there any clues to the timing of this letter?

Can you get a sense of why Paul wrote to the church of Philippi?

How does he feel about the Philippians?

For most of us, being in prison would be a real "Joy Taker". Perhaps that is stating the obvious, but what is Paul's mindset as he writes this letter? Be specific and answer from Scripture.

Now examine your own circumstances **even though** they may be rough right now. Health issues, physical limitations, emotional battles, or any number of other situations might be imprisoning you. Are you allowing the conditions you are facing to steal your joy? List the areas of your life that are "Joy Takers" and submit your feelings about them to God. It's okay to be honest – God knows and He cares.

Joy Is Being Found a Pencil

Happiness is finding a pencil or so sings Charlie Brown after he realizes how human the little red-headed girl is: "I'm so happy. That little red-headed girl dropped her pencil. It has teeth marks all over it. She nibbles her pencil. She's human! It hasn't been such a bad day after all."

I'm partial to that part of the song because I am extremely partial to pencils. My most preferred writing tool is the mechanical pencil. One reason I prefer pencils is because they best showcase all the hours of Palmer Method penmanship I practiced in elementary school. Do you remember the Palmer Method of writing? It used to be the most popular handwriting technique before schools decided to do away with cursive. Children have a difficult time reading my writing unless I print, but the older generations will often pay my "pencil written words" the most superior of compliments: "You write just like a nun!"

Even though there are at least nine considerations when choosing the right kind of pencil, it often plays second fiddle to the pen. Legal documents, checks and all kinds of licenses must be signed in ink. Plus, you know you have matured as a child when the day comes that you trade in your pencils for pens. It is like a rite of passage declaring for all to see that you have become a capable expert who makes few, if any, mistakes while scribing letters into words and sentences. The underlying message is that grown-ups use pens, not pencils.

That may be so, but God (who never makes any mistakes) often chooses to use pencils. At least that's what Mother Teresa claimed. During an interview many years ago, Mother Teresa was asked if she felt she had any special qualities or if she felt it was an extraordinary thing to be a vehicle of God's grace in the world. Her reply was that all the work she was doing was His work and that God wants to show His greatness by using nothingness. "I don't think so. I don't claim anything of the work. It is His work. I am like a little pencil in his hand. That is all. He does the thinking. He does the writing. The pencil has nothing to do with it. The pencil has only to be allowed to be used. In human terms, the success of our work should not have happened."

I bet Mother Teresa excelled at Palmer Method and wrote just like a nun! Indeed, happiness is finding a pencil, but joy is being found a pencil in the hand of God. (Sheryl)

> **"But now, O LORD, You are our Father,**
> **We are the clay, and You our potter;**
> **And all of us are the work of Your hand."**
> **Isaiah 64:8**

Week One

Day 3

"I shall delight myself in Your statutes; I shall not forget Your Word."
Psalm 119:16

Do we truly delight in the Word of God? Let's ask Him to help us retain all the truths we are learning as we study this day.

To really understand the book of Philippians, we have to back-track and look at the life of Paul in the book of Acts. Read Acts 15:36 through Acts 17:1 and answer the following questions. This is Paul's second missionary journey and if you have a map in your Bible, it might interest you to trace this route.

How did Paul and Timothy meet?

How was Timothy described?

Why did they go to Philippi?

Is there any record of a synagogue in Philippi?

Where did they worship?

What happened there and why is it significant?

Describe what happened next from Acts 16:18-40.

What were Paul and Silas doing while in jail?

Did their behavior have any effect on anyone there?

Consider the far reaching effects of Paul's ministry. It's reaching us right now! One man determined and dedicated to the cause of Christ with God's leading changed the world. Was it easy? Not at all. Was his life a continuous "feast of joy"? Not at all. Record any additional insights about Paul, your circumstances, the joy you have in Christ and the passion you possess for Him.

Optional Assignment: If you have time, read the rest of the book of Acts (chapters 20-28) As you read ask God to give you a feel for this man, Paul – his passion, his determination, his heartaches, and his joys.

Can you relate to any of his circumstances? Can you, with Paul, decide to press on toward the goal of knowing Him despite the cost?

Week One

Day 4

⟨decorative flourish⟩

"Make me understand the way of Your precepts,
so I will meditate on Your wonders."
Psalm 119:27

*L*et's ask God to give us a real sense of His wonders so that we will understand His ways.

Many times in his writings, Paul identifies himself as a bondservant of the Lord. That is certainly not a word we hear in our everyday conversation. The English transliteration for the Greek word bondservant is "doulos". What did Paul mean when he said he was a bondservant? What would using this term mean for his readers? What could it mean for us today?

The picture of a bondservant is first found in the Old Testament. After six years of service to the master, a slave was given his (or her) freedom in the seventh year. A slave who chose of his own free will to remain and serve his master assumed the role of a bondservant. To further understand the process involved, read Deuteronomy 15:12-18 and summarize the first four verses in this passage.

What three reasons are given for wanting to remain a servant? (vs. 16)

How long then would one remain a bondservant? (vs. 17)

How was a bondservant "marked"? (vs. 17)

Look up Galatians 6:17 and see how Paul describes being "marked".

Obviously, the readers of Paul's letters would know immediately what he meant by being a bondservant. They would understand his devotion and commitment to Jesus as his Master and Lord. Can we now extend that definition to our own lives? From the following cross references, let's make application of what it means for us to be a bondservant of Christ.

John 13:1-5, 14-15

1 Corinthians 4:1-6

1 Corinthians 6:19-20

Galatians 1:10

Proper application of Scripture is vital to our Christian walk. However, for some people this task proves to be most difficult. With enough prayer and practice we will find ourselves growing in our ability to read the Word and apply it correctly to our lives. Thinking about everything we have learned about being a bondservant, let's write out at least three personal applications using statements of actions or commitments and the pronoun "I". Here are some examples:

"I will be a servant of Jesus and follow his example."

"I will be found faithful."

List yours here:

Now let's carry this exercise a bit further by making it even more personal:

"I will be a servant of Jesus and follow His example by_____
_____."

"I will be found faithful at home or at work when_____
_____."

"I will _____."

Writing out these "I will" statements will cause us to solidify and personalize what we've learned by studying the Scriptures on our own. Let's ask God to lead us in our thinking and be **will**ing to bend our will to His perfect plan for our lives.

"I Wish That I Had…"

My favorite Dr. Suess book (written under the name Theo LeSieg) is "I Wish That I Had Duck Feet". It's a fanciful tale of a little boy who just longs to have an extra special feature that would make him different or stand out in the crowd. He starts with duck feet, considers a whale spout, ponders a long tail and even tries on an elephant's nose. However, for all the advantages each one of these attributes brings, there's a disadvantage. After all, if he actually had an elephant's nose, his dad would surely make him wash the windows or the car! The rhymes from this book are still stuck in my head and it may be because like that little boy, I had a teacher named Miss Banks. When he has the whale spout, Miss Banks thanks him for keeping the "school so cool".

The narrator's problem resonates with us no matter what our age. If we are willing to admit it, sometimes we have a longing to be special, to be noticed – to be unique in our abilities and talents. It seems that when we look around at what others can do and start comparing, we fall short on our own measuring scale – but how does God see us?

In the first chapter of Philippians, Paul tells the church in Philippi, this great and encouraging truth.

> **"For I am confident of this very thing,**
> **that He who began a good work in**
> **you will perfect it until the day of Christ Jesus."**
> **Philippians 1:6**

Comparing ourselves physically or spiritually with others can be a real Joy Taker. Although there is a common master design – we are all fearfully and wonderfully made (see Psalm 139:14) – our individual designs are diverse and varied. He gifted each one of us in a way suited for His purposes. Once we submit our lives to Him, He will continue perfecting or completing His plan. We may look around and get a little frustrated or impatient. We may even be tempted to try out some duck feet or a whale spout, but they won't "fit" for very long. At the end the book, the little boy realizes it is best to be himself.

Perhaps we should consider that thought, but join with it this prayer: "Lord, you made me in your image, You designed me with intent and purpose. You have plans for me that only I can accomplish. Help me not to focus on what I perceive as my 'have-nots', but to trust You to finish the good work you started in me."

A simple truth from a children's book can be a real Joy Maker! (Cammy)

"Joy is the gigantic secret
of the Christian life."
- G.K. Chesterton

Week Two

Introduction

The book of Acts fills in many colorful details of Paul's life. From beatings to shipwrecks to snakebites, Paul endured far more than we can imagine facing. However, toward the end of his life, in defense of his position before King Agrippa, Paul states, "I am standing trial for the hope of the promise made by God..." (Acts 26:6)

Standing trial for hope... what if you were on trial for "hope of the promise"? Would you have a case? Could you be convicted? Is there enough evidence of true joy in your life to defend your position?

Over the next few days, we will look at each chapter of Philippians with the mindset of identifying "Joy Takers". Our goal will be to find the antidote to these circumstances that rob us of our true joy. We will label these spiritual principles "Joy Makers". As you read through the book of Philippians, keep these questions in mind:

What robs me of my joy?

What truths can I learn from Scripture and place firmly in my grasp to combat these Joy Takers in my life?

Week Two

Day 1

"I shall run the way of Your commandments,
for You will enlarge my heart."
Psalm 119:32

*C*an you imagine running after the commandments of God? Can you imagine being so excited that you couldn't just walk toward them, but you wanted to chase after His Words? Ask God to give you that kind of desire for His Word so that He can enlarge your heart.

Last week we spent the bulk of our study time looking back at Paul's life. Today we want to see what we can learn about the people who received this letter. Read through Philippians 1 (just the first chapter) and mark all the references to the recipients. If you are choosing not to mark your Bible, just read through the text and make careful notes. See if you can answer the questions listed below and also jot down anything you see that could be a possible Joy Taker either for Paul or the Philippians.

Who were the Philippians? In other words how were they described? Hint: in verse 7, they are called "partakers of grace". What does this tell you about them?

What were their circumstances?

How did Paul feel about them?

What was their role in the gospel message?

Note: Many people feel this type of exercise is "mechanical". It is true that you might get caught up in the details of finding all the pronouns related to marking a certain people group. However, what you are doing by slowing down and reading the text like this is actually helping you to absorb the Word of God in a different way. Taking the time to ask questions will aid you in thinking critically about the text and help you accurately interpret the passage when it is time to make application.

If you like to mark key words in the Scriptures, now would be a good time to also mark the following words: gospel, joy/rejoice, prayer and Jesus Christ.

Notice how Paul prays for the Philippians 1:4.

Read verses 9-11 of chapter 1 and list Paul's "requests" for the Philippians.

Is there anyone in your life that could use more love or real knowledge and discernment? What about you? Could you use more love and knowledge?

Do you need to pray that someone you know will "approve the things that are excellent"?

Do you think neglecting to pray for ourselves and those we love could be labeled a Joy Taker?

Spend some time reflecting on that thought as your end your study time today.

Week Two

Day 2

"Establish Your word to Your servant as
that which produces reverence for you."
Psalm 119:35

*A*sk God to establish His word deep in your soul to help you identify the Joy Takers in your life.

Have you ever had your joy stolen? It can happen so quickly – a phone call, a text message, running into someone at the store who has bad news. Other times, it seems to sneak up on you. Everything seems to be going well, but you lose a bit of focus and before long you find yourself feeling somewhat depleted in the joy department.

Circumstances are One of life's biggest Joy Stealers. Paul certainly could list (and he often did!) all the situations that could have taken his joy away and changed his perspective on his mission in life. However, Paul had a different outlook. Read Philippians 1:12-26 and answer the following questions.

Where is Paul at the time of this writing?

What was he facing there that could steal his joy?

Instead of letting his circumstances rule his emotions, what was his passion? Go back to the text for your answer.

What is his attitude toward the fact that Christ is being preached "from envy and strife"?

Is there any indication false doctrine is being preached?

How did Paul keep his perspective?

Placing the facts of a situation over our feelings is one of the most difficult disciplines in the Christian walk. Please understand I am not dismissing our healthy God-given emotions. However, we must be willing and able to examine how we "feel" and line up the proven facts we know to guide us then in the proper response.

Spend the rest of your time today studying Psalm 143. I call this particular Psalm "The Woman's Psalm" because it seems to sum up how it feels to be spiraling out of control emotionally. The beauty of this passage though is that it offers a prescription for the over-whelmed soul. Hint: there are three things listed to do in verse 5. Record your insights and comments below and what you learn about "fact over feelings" from the Psalm.

UPDATE YOUR JOY SOFTWARE

If you've heard the rumor about me, it's true. I've crossed over to the world of e-readers! If you own an e-reader, you know how difficult it is to keep pace with the latest version of software. One Christmas, when the battle of the latest improved digital readers took place, e-reader users could upgrade to a new version of software that would keep us current without having to upgrade to a brand new device. Not a bad deal!

The upgrade could be done manually for those who enjoy immediate gratification or it would come in time as the great wizard of technology would update over a period of a few weeks. Of course, Cammy got her upgrade right away while I waited patiently for it to automatically appear, but alas, days grew into weeks – and nothing! I called wizard headquarters in the land of e-reader Oz only to be told to wait just a little longer because "the mind of the software isn't thinking right" and a few bugs needed to be worked out it so as to prevent a wonky reading experience.

That experience made me think about joy, partly because not having the latest Nook upgrade was less than joyful for me. I didn't want to have to wait patiently for the newest and best, but my attitude reminded me that it was not just my e-reader software that needed an upgrade. My "joy software" needed one too because my mind, like the mind of the Nook software, wasn't "thinking right". However, to experience all that true joy has to offer we must first improve the quality of our thinking.

In **Philippians 4:8**, Paul made it very clear as to what and how we are to work out the bugs in our thinking:

"Finally, brethren, whatever is true, whatever is honorable, whatever is right, whatever is pure, whatever is lovely, whatever is of good repute, if there is any excellence and if anything worthy of praise, dwell on these things."

Someone once said, "Those who experience more joy don't necessarily have more to be joyful about; they just think differently." Part of thinking differently involves thinking with a **Philippians 4:8** mentality. Every thought focus in this verse is positive: true, honorable, pure, lovely, of good repute, excellent and worthy of praise. Part of upgrading our joy software so that we "think right" is to focus on positive thoughts and rid our minds of the negative bugs. As children of God we are called to be good stewards of our thought life and not to fill our minds with things that go against His law and desires "so that you will prove yourselves to be blameless and innocent, children of God above reproach in the midst of a crooked and perverse generation, among whom you appear as lights in the world…" **(Philippians 2:15).**

Everything we choose to download or upload to our minds – what we read, watch, listen to and even who we choose to associate with – can either nudge us further away or bring us closer to joy. When we are upgraded closer to joy, we will shine like the stars in the universe to others who are "reading" our lives. That's much better than a software upgrade any day! (Sheryl)

Week Two

Day 3

"Behold, I long for Your precepts;
revive me through your righteousness."
Psalm 119:40

As you study today, ask God to reveal truth about His righteousness to you so that you can be revived.

My grandmother had many "grandmotherly" sayings, but one of them was truly unusual. Before any of us (granddaughters or grandsons) would leave to go on a date or to a ball game, she would stand on the porch and wave to us while calling out, "Be Pretty!" That was her way of telling us to behave.

Paul gives a charge to the Philippians in Philippians 1:27. Write out the verse and what you think he was telling them to do.

Did you happen to notice a connector in that verse? Two little words: "so that". Paul is basically saying "Be pretty so that whether I can come see you or not, I don't have to worry about you behaving!"

Can you think of a Joy Taker associated with this concept?

Let me offer this one: Being caught unprepared or misbehaving is a major Joy Taker. Paul hoped to get back and visit the Philippians, but he didn't know if a physical visit to Philippi could be a reality. However, the Philippians' behavior needed to be consistent no matter if he made the visit or not. They should always be ready.

Can you think of a time you were caught "unprepared"? What did that do to your joy meter? From the following passages, describe ways we can stay alert and be ready or in the words of my grand-mother: "Be pretty!"

Matthew 24:42-46

Galatians 6:7-10

1 Peter 1:13-19

Now, be practical. What do you need to change about your daily routine so that at any given moment you can be found in "a manner worthy of the gospel of Christ"?

Week Two

Day 4

"It was good for me that I was afflicted,
that I may learn Your statutes."
Psalm 119:71

$\mathcal{I}$f we were truly honest, we might be willing to admit there are verses in the Bible we wish were just not there. Philippians 1:29 would probably fall into that category. The topic of suffering is difficult to study and there is no way to make it palatable. Oswald Chambers had this to say about suffering: "We all know people who have been made much meaner and more irritable and more intolerable to live with by suffering; it is not right to say all suffering perfects. It only perfects one type of person... the one who accepts the call of God in Christ Jesus."

Before you begin your study today, read the prayer starter again. With that verse fresh in your mind, write out Philippians 1:29 in the space provided.

Now, without gauging your reaction or trying to be "spiritual", jot down how reading that verse makes you feel.

When approaching a subject like suffering, the best way to under-stand the implications of what it means to suffer is to look at as many verses as possible related to the theme. The following list of Scriptures is in no way exhaustive, even though you might find it exhausting! Study what you can with an open heart and a mind open to God's plan for your life – a plan that will include suffering.

John 15:18-21

Romans 5:3-5

Romans 8:16-18

2 Corinthians 4:11-18

Hebrews 2:10

1 Peter 1:6-9

1 Peter 2:19-25

1 Peter 3:8-14, 17

1 Peter 4:12-14

1 Peter 5:10

After carefully examining the Word of God, how should we respond to suffering in our lives? It might be helpful to make a list of all the truths you learned about suffering.

"Be Pretty"

While I was growing up in Mississippi, my grandmother (my dad's mom) lived two doors down from me. When I say, I "beat a path" to her house, I did just literally that. There was a visible path through the grass worn down by my bare feet from my front door to hers. Memories can be tricky, but I seem to remember she was almost always in the kitchen when I ran through her screen door. For sure I know that every single time I left her house, she was standing on the front porch, waving goodbye and watching me run back home.

Her name was Alice Beatrice, but to her 13 grandchildren she was "Mamaw Bea" and she was very "grandmotherly". Since I lived the closest to her, I popped in and out of her house at will, but without fail, she would watch me leave and if she knew I was leaving her house to go somewhere else besides back home, she would call out one of her most unique "grandmotherly" sayings, "BE PRETTY!" That was Mamaw Bea's way of telling me to behave. In her presence I had to behave, but she wanted me to "be pretty" whether she was with me or not!

In **Philippians 1:27**, we find Paul writing something along those lines to the church at Philippi.

> **"Only conduct yourselves in a manner worthy of the gospel of Christ, so that whether I come and see you or remain absent, I will hear of you that you are standing firm in one spirit, with one mind striving together for the faith of the gospel."**

Maybe my grandmother was echoing Paul's words when he said, "Be pretty so that whether I can come see you or not, I don't have to worry about you behaving!" Being caught misbehaving is a major joy stealer. See, I grew up in a small town – any misconduct on my part reflected on my family and the news would spread pretty quickly. At any given moment, someone could see me and report to my parents or my grandmother. They always wanted to hear that I was "standing firm" on the principles they had instilled in me as a child. It would have stolen their joy (and mine later!) to hear that I was not behaving.

Paul's exhortation to the Philippians is about more than "behaving" – it's about being united in one mind striving for the faith of the gospel. He wanted the Philippians to do more than have proper conduct; he wanted their actions to reflect their changed hearts. The church at Philippi was new and they were pointing people to the risen Christ. For many unbelievers, it would begin with noticing that these Philippians were behaving ChristLIKE.

Think about your daily routine and all the people who see you at your work or school or business – how would they say you "behave"? Like Christ? As **1 Peter 1:15** says, "As obedient children, do not be conformed to the former lusts which were yours in ignorance, but (be) like the Holy One who called you, be holy yourselves in all your behavior."

Or in the words of my grandmother, "BE PRETTY!" (Cammy)

"If you have no joy,
there's a leak in your Christianity somewhere."
-Billy Sunday

Week Three

Introduction

When my daughter was younger, we tried to help her understand the importance of obedience with a little rhyming question and answer routine. We would ask, "Now how do you obey?" She was supposed to respond by saying:

All the way
Right away
And with a happy heart

Well, it doesn't really rhyme, but it has a nice cadence. The point of teaching her this little ditty was to show that obedience is not truly complete without the proper attitude. We may "obey", but if we do it grudgingly, we are not honoring God or the person who asked us for a show of obedience. Attitude matters. In fact, it is key and although we cannot control someone else's attitude, we can certainly learn to manage our own.

This week we will study the attitude of Christ in Philippians 2. We will look at His humility, His love and His willingness to set aside everything to come to earth and be a sacrifice for our sins. As you study this week, be very aware of your own attitude. What are the situations and/or people who cause you to be impatient, frustrated or lose your temper? Do you face each and every day expecting the worst possible scenario, or do you live in a state of expectation watching for God's hand at work? Is your attitude a Joy Taker? Perhaps we all could use an attitude adjustment.

Week Three

Day 1

"The law of Your mouth is better to me
than thousands of gold and silver pieces."
Psalm 119:72

Would you mind taking a moment to be conscious of what you are holding in your hand or lap? You have available to you the entire counsel of God - God breathed, inspired and complete. Not only is it accessible, you can study it openly without fear of being arrested or imprisoned. How much is this book worth to you – more than "thousands of gold and silver pieces"? Praise Him for allowing you the privilege of having His Word.

Your study time today will be spent mainly observing Philippians 2. Read through Philippians 2 slowly and out loud if you can. If you are marking in your Bible, continue to mark these words from the previous chapter:

the Philippians
joy/rejoice
gospel
Jesus Christ

It might be helpful to read chapter 2 more than once as you highlight these words and concepts. You can also add the words mind/attitude to your list.

Read through the chapter again and write down any Joy Takers you see.

In the very beginning of chapter 2, Paul makes a request of the Philippians. He writes to them, "make my joy complete". As we have already discussed, joy is a gift from God and true joy is something that only believers can know. Paul is not asking the Philippians to give him the gift of joy, but to complete or fill up to the brim, his joy. It is clear from his words that there are a couple of things that the saints at Philippi could do that would add to his already joyful state.

Read Philippians 2:2 and discover the "Joy Makers" which Paul says would "make my joy complete."

Paul cherished unity and sameness. In essence, his joy was most full when "likeness of mind" existed among the Philippians. However, it is safe to say that if something has the potential to make joy, something else has the potential to steal joy. What are those things that cause a congregation, friends or families to lack unity or to lack "likeness of mind"?

Now read Philippians 2:3 and capture yet another "Joy Maker" for Paul. What is it and what would it look like?

Is Paul saying that we can never look on our own interests?

"Likeness of mind" and "lowliness of mind" were significant "Joy Makers" for Paul. Again, we must be aware that while something can complete joy, something else can subtract joy. John 10:10 tells us that Satan, the thief, "comes only to steal..." so how is it that "lowliness of mind" can be stolen? What interferes with it?

Week Three

Day 2

"Forever, O Lord, Your word is settled in heaven."
Psalm 119:89

God's Word is settled forever in heaven and our salvation was settled forever at the foot of the cross. Today, as you study Jesus and His attitude toward becoming man and facing the cross, ask God to give you a fresh look at His word and to settle it deep in your heart. For a quick recap, briefly summarize in your own words, Philippians 2:1-4.

According to Philippians 2:5, whose attitude are we to have?

Of course the next question is, "What does this look like?" The next few verses are often called "one of the greatest passages in the Word of God on the Incarnation of Jesus Christ." Here we see Christ's humility, His majesty, His love, and His obedience and we are challenged to consider our own humility and obedience. From Philippians 2:6-11 answer the following questions just using just the text for your answers.

What does verse 6 teach about Christ before He came to earth as a man?

What had to happen for Jesus to take on human form? (vs. 7)

What does this passage tell us about Christ's obedience? (vs. 8)

What attitude was necessary for this type of extreme obedience? (vs. 8)

How did God respond to the obedience of His Son? (vs. 9-11)

Now, let's make it personal. How does this knowledge help us in our attempts to maintain an attitude of humility?

Lack of humility can definitely be a joy stealer. Can you think of another word for the term "lack of humility"?

Just to clarify what the Bible says about humility, check the following references:

Proverbs 15:33

Isaiah 57:15

Matthew 20:26-27

James 4:4-6

Hebrews 2 will help you pull all these thoughts together. Read Hebrews 2:14-18. Think carefully through these verses and apply them to your life. He was made like His brethren "in all things" so He could fully identify will all our struggles. When you are working hard to set yourself aside for others, how does this knowledge about Jesus comfort you?

Let the full impact of this truth sink deeply into your mind and your soul. Imagine standing at the foot of the cross and "behold the Lamb of God" who willingly gave His life for you. Watch Christ and sense His attitude. Entreat Him to help you fully realize what it is to have this mind, this attitude that was also in Christ Jesus.

"If the Son of God had gone from incarnation to the cross without a life of temptation and pain to test his righteousness and love, He would not be a suitable Savior for fallen man."

John Piper, *Fifty Reasons Jesus Came to Die*

"IN it or ON it?"

Sheryl and I often say when we are out teaching together, "Words matter and God's Word matters most." It's a true statement and one lesson about words I've learned recently is not to overlook even the smallest ones.

My son was home for a couple of days between his January term at college and the beginning of the spring semester. His "J-term" class that year was theology and just as I imagined, he really enjoyed learning about the founding fathers of church history. Wednesday night while sitting next to me on the couch in a "college break semi coma mode", he mumbled, "I learned a lot of really big words in theology class." Of course I wanted to know what they were and he said, "Um... Homoousian and some Filioque Clause". He didn't bother to explain what either of these terms meant and to be honest I sure didn't know, but by then he had drifted back off to sleep and my mind had drifted back to two words I had pondered that morning.

My words are not so big or impressive but I think they matter. My two words?

IN and ON

As we continue to study Philippians and examine the reason for Paul's ability to remain joyful no matter what his circumstances (the shipwrecks, the snakebites, the stonings; oh my!) it seems to me that one of the secrets to his success is found in the difference between these two little words. Paul's joy was found IN the Lord not just ON Him. Let me offer a couple of very simplified examples.

If I place a picture or a reminder note ON my refrigerator, as I often do, the refrigerator is serving a purpose. However, if I put an item IN the refrigerator, whatever I put there enjoys all the benefits of the reason for the appliance. Namely, it gets cold and won't spoil. The taste will be enhanced or it will stay fresher longer.

If I go to the pool in the summer and lie ON a float, I'm near the water, but not really IN it. However, hopping off of the float into the water to swim, I will be fully immersed and once again, enjoy all its benefits. Namely I get cool and wet.

Paul's outlook of steadfast joy was based on a steadfast confidence

IN the Lord. He was enjoying all the benefits to be had by being fully encompassed and immersed in God's presence and trusting IN His promises. Thus Paul's ability to say, **"Finally, my brethren, rejoice IN the Lord. To write the same things again is no trouble to me, and it is a safeguard to you" (Philippians 3:1).**

As I considered my little word "IN" compared to my son's big, important-sounding college theology words, I realized a very common catchphrase right now encases the word and captures the essence completely. The phrase is "living intentionally". It is a worthy concept and one that I want to change to "living IN-tentionally". No matter what circumstances you find yourself IN – a shipwreck of faith, the stones of harsh words thrown at you by another, or the snakebite of betrayal, I pray you will place your faith IN the fullness and completeness offered by the Lord. May your goal be to enjoy all the benefits of living IN-tentionally IN Him. (Cammy)

"...For IN Him, all things hold together..."
Colossians 1:17

Week Three

Day 3

"I will never forget Your precepts, for by them You have revived me."
Psalm 119:93

Just as we sometimes come across passages of Scripture we wish just were not there (like the ones on suffering), we also sometimes find verses that are difficult to understand. Philippians 2:12-13 might be a good example of "difficult to understand". Is the Bible saying I have to work out my salvation? What does "with fear and trembling" mean? Today you will understand how useful word studies are to learning more about the Bible. Just from those two verses, answer the following questions:

Who is supposed to do the work in verse 12?

Who is working in verse 13?

Write the word that follows the word "work" in verse 12.

What two words follow the word "work" in verse 13?

Can you write a summary statement from answering those questions? I will get you started:

Man's responsibility is to _____ _____ what God _____ _____.

Now, very carefully, using just the same two verses, (Philippians 2:12-13) answer these questions:

What is God working in us?

Why?

How are we to work out our salvation? (vs. 12)

What do you think this means?

To fully and completely understand what it means to work out your salvation with fear and trembling, a few word definitions are given below. Read these definitions carefully in the context of those verses and see if it helps your understanding.

Work out – original word: "katergazomai" (vs. 12)
    To perform or achieve, to do something that produces results

Fear – original word: "phobos" (vs. 12)
    Fear, dread, reverence as for a husband
    A wholesome dread of displeasing God
    A constant carefulness when dealing with others

At work – original word: "energeo" (vs. 13)
    To put forth power, to aid

With a better understanding of what these two verses mean, look up Ephesians 4:29-32 and see if you can make any connections. Do you see any Joy Takers in this passage?

Week Three

Day 4

"How sweet are Your words to my taste! Yes,
sweeter than honey to my mouth!"
Psalm 119:103

*W*ARNING: Do NOT complete today's study if you ever intend to grumble or complain again. Consider yourself duly warned and if you are still there, time to get started.

Your first assignment is to read through the second chapter of Philippians again to restore context in your mind and heart. List below the concepts covered thus far in Chapter 2:

Now, write out in your own words what Philippians 2:14-15 is saying.

In Philippians 2:12-13, Paul tells the recipients of his letter to work out their salvation with "fear and trembling". Why would he follow that exhortation with a directive about "grumbling and disputing?"

The free website, www.blueletterbible.org, offers definitions of Biblical terms from the original language. Read the following transliterations and reflect on what Paul is really telling them to do or not to do.

Grumbling (murmurings KJV) – original word: "goggysmos" (vs. 14)
  Murmur, muttering
  A secret debate, a secret pleasure not openly avowed
  Root word – those who discontentedly complain

Disputing – original word: "dialogismos" (vs. 14)
  A deliberating questioning about what is true
  Hesitation, doubting
  Disputing, arguing

With the defining terms in place, how do you read and interpret Philippians 2:14 now?

When we obey verse 14, what is the result? Hint: Make a simple list of what happens in verse 15.

How are grumbling or complaining Joy Takers? Be specific with examples from your own life.

Why would Paul warn the Philippians about grumbling and disputing?

1 Corinthians 10:1-11 is a very interesting and brief history lesson. Read these verses carefully and write out the five things listed in this passage (specifically in verses 6-10) we are **not** to do. Do you see a familiar word?

What were some of the results from these actions?

Since 1 Corinthians referred to the Old Testament, take a look at Exodus 17:1-7. What is found at the root of most, if not all, grumbling?

Record your conclusions below from today's study on grumbling. Can you make any applications for your life?

One more thing: Re-read the prayer starter at the beginning of this lesson. If God's word is sweet as honey in your mouth, what do you think grumbling and disputing words taste like?

Joy Alert

"Joy Alert! Today only! Free shipping and 25% off all items!" In the wee hours of every morning during a recent Christmas season I received emails like this from a popular clothing store. It was as if they were waving a flag to say, "Hey! Shop with us! We have some deals that will make you joyful this season!" While they did have some great deals, and while I did get in on at least one day of a shopping spree with them, the "joy alert" must have expired by day's end because the very next morning a new alert, with even more promising deals would appear.

As much as I benefitted from the shopping deal, I must admit that the alert was more of a happiness alert than a joy alert. It is very common to think that joy and happiness are one and the same and part of that thinking is Charlie Brown's fault. Yes, because even though he was a good man, Charlie Brown taught us that happiness is finding a pencil, pizza with sausage, five different crayons, learning to whistle and tying your shoe for the very first time. Indeed in all of those moments most anybody can be happy, but unlike joy, true Biblical joy, those happy moments are conditional and fleeting at best. What if you never find that pencil or have pizza with sausage? Are you not happy then? What if you lost one or two of your five crayons? Is your happiness then gone? Like the clothing store Joy Alert, happiness frequently expires within a day.

The apostle Paul, while imprisoned and not in such favorable circumstances, wrote the epistle to the Philippians in which he captures what true joy and rejoicing really is! True joy goes beyond having a sister, catching a firefly and setting it free. It is often surrounded by unfavorable and uncomfortable circumstances. Unlike the clothing store flag waving a joy alert for "today only", joy has to do with the flag that waves over the castle of our hearts indicating that Jesus, the King, has taken up residence forever within regardless of what is happening without! (Sheryl)

**"Splendor and majesty are before Him,
Strength and joy are in His place."
1 Chronicles 16:7**

"There is a joy which isn't given to the ungodly,
that of those who love thee for thine own sake,
whose joy thou thyself art; and this is
the happy life to rejoice in thee, and of thee.
This is it and there is none other."
-Augustine

Week Four

Introduction

There is no doubt we live in a goal-oriented society. There are programs available now for preschoolers, who may barely know their primary colors that will begin grooming them for college! We are compelled as a culture and as individuals to set and achieve goals according to the decade or season of our lives. Some of us had the goal to be married by our 20s and have children by our 30s. Some people may have a goal of traveling around the world or to retire before the typical age of 65. It is not a bad thing to have goals because they are usually set for the purpose of improving the quality of our lives, our actions, or our behavior and they are often a window into our hearts. What do your goals reveal about your heart?

What is most precious to you, of the utmost importance? What are your goals, your passions and your ambitions? What have you counted on for your identity? Would you be willing to let go of it for the sake of Jesus Christ and His kingdom? These are probing questions indeed. As we dig deeper into Philippians 3 this week, we will learn where Paul placed his confidence, what his life goal was and how he strived to achieve that goal.

What about you? Where are you placing your confidence? Could this be a snare or a Joy Taker for you? Do your goals bring you joy or do you find the things you want to achieve are robbing you of great joy? Keep those thoughts in mind as you study this week.

Week Four

Day 1

"Your Word is a lamp to my feet and a light to my path."
Psalm 119:105

Pray today that the Lord will illuminate His Word to you in a way that you will find yourself walking with confidence in the light of His glory and grace.

You might be able to guess what today's work will encompass. Yes – observing and marking (if you are choosing to do so) Philippians 3. Read through the chapter slowly and out loud if possible. Try to absorb the content and context of this chapter in the framework of Philippians 1-4. If you find yourself asking questions as you read, jot them down in the margins of your notes.

Earlier you were asked to mark all the references to Paul throughout the entire book. As you read through the third chapter of Philippians, pay close attention to these markings and to what Paul is saying about himself. It would be very helpful at this point to make a list of what you learn about Paul from Chapter 3. Who is he? What was his background?

Now, write out some thoughts or reflections you have on this chapter.

There's a phrase in Philippians 3:3-4 you may have noticed. Paul uses the term "confidence in the flesh" three times. Looking at the context of these verses, Philippians 3:1-7, what do you think Paul means?

Time to put on your thinking cap. Based on the list of what Paul could have put his confidence in – for example, his religious upbringing – can you find any modern day parallels for churchgoers today?

How could placing your confidence in the flesh be a Joy Taker?

In what do you place your confidence? Be honest and sincere before the Lord.

Week Four

Day 2

"I have inherited Your testimonies forever,
for they are the joy of my heart."
Psalm 119:111

Are the testimonies of God the joy of your heart? Does studying His word bring you great joy? It is our prayer that you are growing to love His Word and find great joy in His Presence.

Even though Paul never referred to himself as a "teacher" he very well could have in Philippians 3 because, like any good teacher, Paul was willing to repeat himself. Paul begins the chapter by saying in verse 1 that "to write the same things again is no trouble to me." Why? Because these reminders are a "safeguard" for them… something that is certain and true and can be relied upon to guard their minds and hearts. Paul continues in verse 2 with some warnings—he was very specific about the dangers surrounding the people he loved.

What were the three things the Philippians were to "beware of"? List them here:

The first warning Paul gave in verse 2 was to beware of the dogs. In the Greek "dog" literally means what first comes to our minds... the adorable four-legged animal that is man's best friend. However, in the Greek "dog" is also a metaphor for a man of "impure mind". Paul had all kinds of people following him around; some were harmless, but others were dangerous because they attempted to pervert and distort the gospel of grace that Paul preached. When he issued the warning, "beware of the dogs", he was referring to the men "nipping at his heels" and "barking" their false teachings. (See Isaiah 56:10-12.)

The evil workers in verse two could also mean false teachers and include those who disguised themselves as apostles of Christ. (See 2 Corinthians 11:13.) That brings us to the third "beware". What's all this about circumcision? The only way to understand what Paul meant in these verses is to go back to the Old Testament. Remember, Scripture will always interpret Scripture and when we find a passage that is confusing, the first step is to see if it is mentioned elsewhere in the Bible. We will find the first mention of circumcision in Genesis 17 when God confirmed His covenant with Abraham. At that point, God instituted the practice of circumcision with Abraham and if we read the text we will see it extended to his entire family.

A key verse to know is Genesis 15:6: "Then he (Abram) believed in the Lord; and He (the Lord) reckoned it him (Abraham) as righteousness." Abraham believed God **before** the act of circumcision. For Abraham and his family, circumcision was an outward sign of devotion to God. For generations afterward, the Jews taught that circumcision was essential to salvation. However, Paul claimed that circumcision itself (just the physical act) is not necessary, but we must experience a "spiritual circumcision" in Christ. (See Colossians 2:11.) The false teachers (the dogs and evil workers) were trying to get the people back under the Law by demanding that the Gentiles be circumcised in order to be saved.

In Philippians 3:3, Paul says those who are of the "true circumcision" are the ones who put no "confidence in the flesh". Knowing the historical and cultural background of circumcision, what do you think this means?

Paul was telling the saints to beware of physical rites that had not value unless they corresponded to a spiritual experience. In other words, the physical act of circumcision does not save people from their sins. God is not interested in the circumcision of the flesh; He is interested in the circumcision of our hearts. He wants us to have hearts after the Spirit and not after the flesh. Although I may undergo a fleshly rite, if my heart is after the things of the flesh, then what happened to me physically has no bearing on my relationship with God.

Now read Romans 2:25-29. What does this tell you about circumcision?

Can you think of any church or social traditions that occur today that people might put their confidence in as the Jews did with circumcision and thereby, miss the true significance?

One final passage and then you can let your brain rest. Read Romans 4:3-13 and record any final reflections on circumcision and righteousness that is found by faith.

Lose Count

My most favorite math skill, probably the only one I truly enjoy and use every day of my life, is the skill of counting. I love to count things and I love for things I do to count. For example, I love to count how many days there are until Christmas vacation and I like for my good deeds to count. In other words, I like for my neighbors to notice when I scrape the ice and snow off their cars. At those times, I'm tempted to just leave a little ice patch in the corner of their windshield where I can carve, "Cleaned by Sheryl" and then receive the credit for my act of kindness. Counting and having things count are real Joy Makers for me.

Recently I was on a business trip to Orlando, Florida where most flights are like daycare facilities in the sky, with tons of noisy, excited children on board. This trip, however, I only counted a handful of kids on the flight, which made for a very peaceful trip. That was a real Joy Maker.

Usually, when departing from the Orlando airport, the security lines are as long as the theme park lines except without the fast pass option. That's a real Joy Taker, so counting can come in handy. This trip I did a quick head count of the lines, located the shortest line, got in it, and joyfully prepared to speed right through security. That was a real Joy Maker.

Well on my way to beating a path through security check in record time, with only three people in front of me (did I mention how much I enjoy counting?), the x-ray machine went down and the only record I broke that day was for the longest wait in line ever and in any airport I have ever been. That was a real Joy Taker.

When I finally boarded the plane, I offered to give up my aisle seat near the front so a family could sit together. I have to admit that I wouldn't have minded if the flight attendant, right before reviewing the emergency procedures, recounted my good deed to all of the passengers. That would have been a real Joy Maker.

From what I have read about the Apostle Paul, he seemed to enjoy counting too. However, his method of counting doesn't look anything like mine. Right in the middle of listing the number of times he was beaten with rods and shipwrecked (**2 Corinthians 11:25**) and right after carefully itemizing an impressive pedigree in Philippians 3 (a Hebrew of Hebrews, a Pharisee, blameless), Paul lost count! Anything that was tallied in the plus column was then counted as loss for the sake of Christ:

> **"But whatever things were gain to me, those things I have counted as loss for the sake of Christ. More than that, I count all things to be loss in view of the surpassing value of knowing Christ Jesus my Lord, for whom I have suffered the loss of all things, and count them but rubbish so that I may gain Christ..." (Philippians 3:7-8)**

I will never be able to match numbers with Paul concerning all he did and suffered for the Lord, but I can learn the correct way to count from him. The sum total of all of my gain = total loss for the sake of Christ. To count correctly, I must lose count. In the future I may give up more seats on planes and I may clean many a windshield in the neighborhood – but I'll never tell! (Sheryl)

Week Four

Day 3

"The unfolding of Your words gives light;
it gives understanding to the simple."
Psalm 119:130

*L*et's ask the Lord to unfold His Word before us today and give us deep understanding.

If we could have confidence in the flesh to save our souls, who better than Paul to boast in the flesh? Read Philippians 3:5-6 and list Paul's pedigree. What are the things Paul did or accomplished in the flesh that are quite impressive?

In the Sermon on the Mount, Jesus said, "Except your righteousness exceeds that of the scribes and the Pharisees, you shall in no wise enter the kingdom of heaven" (Matthew 5:20). Paul was the poster child for this verse! As far as the righteousness of the scribes and Pharisees, Paul had it. He had done everything that he was supposed to do according to the law to be righteous. In fact, he had gone beyond. He was a Pharisee. He persecuted the church. As far as his zeal and according to the righteousness that is in the law, he was blameless. Still, that is not enough to gain a main entrance into the kingdom of heaven.

The key to all of us coming to Christ is relationship and **not** religion. It is not about keeping the Ten Commandments, getting baptized or circumcised, or doing several random acts of kindness daily. That is religion and not relationship. If religious rites could save, then the shedding of blood by Christ was unnecessary.

In Philippians 3 the word "things" is repeated several times in verses 7-8. Looking back at those verses, what do you think Paul meant when he used the word "things"?

What did those "things" used to be for him? (vs. 7)

What are they now? (vs. 7)

How did this happen? (vs. 7)

What is Paul's outlook on life according to verse 8? Try rewriting that verse in your own words as a prayer to God.

Can "things" – even good "things" –become Joy Takers? If so, how?

With all that you have learned in mind, read Philippians 3:1-14 again. What was Paul's goal in life? Don't just state it. Define it.

If doing physical things could account for righteousness, Paul could have topped anybody. He was circumcised the old fashioned way, on the eighth day and not at age 30 or 40. He was of the tribe of Benjamin. That was a good boast because they were a faithful tribe. He was a Pharisee and the son of a Pharisee and in the law, he was blameless. People would have looked at Paul and said he was righteous.

Paul also cornered the market in keeping the law, but all of that gain to him was counted loss to Christ. His righteousness was not in the law, but in his faith in Christ. If anything in religion could open the door to relationship between God and man, Paul would have been the first one to go through that door. However, religion and religious practices do not save. Only the Lamb of God saves!

What are the goals in **your** life? State them in a list, in concrete terms. Don't rush this exercise and don't feel pressured to give the Sunday School answer. Next to each goal, write out what it will take to accomplish it.

(Note: All your goals might not seem "spiritual", but remember, we are to do everything to the glory of God. For example, one of your goals might be to receive a college degree. That is a fabulous goal and one you can reach with integrity and with influence along the way. You can be a light for Christ on campus.)

Week Four

Day 4

"Establish my footsteps in Your word, and do not let any iniquity have dominion over me."
Psalm 119:133

Have you ever tried to give someone directions and finally just said, "I'm going there, too. Follow me!" Paul does the spiritual equivalent of that in Philippians 3:17 when he says, "Brethren, join in following my example, and observe those who walk according to the pattern you have in us."

Was it right for Paul to set himself up as an example? Please explain.

Paul offers a contrast in verses 18-19 showing how the "enemies of the cross of Christ" walk. What does this walk look like?

What about you? Can you tell someone, "Hey, follow me as I walk the Christian journey"? The key word there is "walk" and just like the prayer started for today, if your steps are not established in God's word, what will happen if someone follows you?

Your assignment today is to study the following passages while keeping these four questions in mind:

1. How am I walking?
2. Where am I walking?
3. Why am I walking there?
4. Can I tell someone to "walk like me"?

Ephesians 4:1-6

Ephesians 4:17-24

Ephesians 5:15-16

Colossians 1:9-12

Before ending your time today, summarize your thoughts about your "walk" and ask God to keep you on His path walking in a manner worthy of His call on your life.

Great Expectations

A friend of mine and I often joke about lowering our expectations. "Expect nothing," we say, "and then you might be pleasantly surprised!" For some reason, that always makes us laugh, although sometimes a bit ruefully if we have had our hopes dashed or we are facing a difficult situation. However, one morning, these words from the book of Joshua leapt off the page at me: **"Then Joshua said to the people, 'Consecrate yourselves, for tomorrow the Lord will do wonders among you'" (Joshua 3:5)**

The word for "consecrate" means "to sanctify, prepare, or dedicate". I'm not sure exactly what consecrating looked like for the Israelites camped there by the Jordan. Maybe they took a bath, cleaned up around the tent, or put on special clothes, but one thing they knew for sure: God was going to show up the next morning and do a wonder among them! Imagine the anticipation! Did anyone go to sleep that night with lowered expectations?

Then, of course, I wondered – what if I lived like this? What if I took the time every night to prepare for the wonderful, marvelous acts of God in my life the next day? What would I feel or experience? Would I go to sleep with lowered expectations?

Paul's unshakable faith throughout the book of Philippians shows how much and how often he expected God to work wonders. Throughout everything he had experienced and even chained to a Roman guard while writing this epistle, he is reminding the Philippians of their true citizenship and what they can expect.

"For our citizenship is in heaven, and we eagerly await a Savior from there, the Lord Jesus Christ, who by the power that enables Him to bring everything under his control will transform our lowly bodies so they will be like His glorious body." (Philippians 3:20-21)

Paul expected great things from God on a daily basis and he also eagerly awaited the "one day that all would be transformed by the power of Christ." I think that realization and belief was another stone in Paul's foundation of joy.

What am I missing because I am not expecting? What am I am not seeing because I am not looking for God's wonders? What if I went to bed every night anticipating great things the next day? After pondering these verses, I wrote out a little prayer:

"Lord, You do great wonders every moment of every day, from managing the split second timing of the sun's arrival for me to its setting in just the right spot so it is rising for someone else in another part of the world. My heart beats throughout the night, every night, and I am not even aware of it – what a wonder! But what am I missing because I am not anticipating and not consecrating myself at the end of each day? Sanctify this complacent heart of mine and open my mind to receive Your truth. Clear my vision to behold Your wondrous works. Amen." (Cammy)

"Gospel repentance is tapping into the joy of our union with Christ in order to weaken our need to do anything contrary to God's heart."
-Tim Keller

Week Five

Introduction

Scotty Smith, founding pastor of Christ Community Church in Franklin, Tennessee, began posting daily prayers on a blog a couple of years ago. The blog began to attract quite a bit of traffic and eventually all the entries were compiled into a book entitled "Everyday Prayers". His words before the Lord are honest and transparent; his prayers are genuine and revealing. As we study Philippians this week and focus some specific joy takers like worry and discontent, consider this prayer from Scotty's book:

"Jesus, the ache within our hearts for peace is unrelenting. Let me get specific: the ache within my heart is unrelenting. Though I already rest in you plus nothing for my forgiveness and righteousness, I still get sucker punched by the tantalizing illusion that peace can be found in something or someone else."

Can you identify with this ache for peace? Is lack of peace a Joy Taker for you?

"Some days, Jesus, I get lost in the world of "if only". If only there were no tensions in any of my relationships, I'd be a happy man. If only the phone wouldn't ring again, demanding a little more of me than I have to offer, I would be fine. If only I lived somewhere else, worked with different people, had a different body, had more money, had fewer hassles, had a different spouse, had never been deeply wounded, were twenty years younger..."

Do these words "if only" resonate with you? Have you found yourself caught up in the maelstrom of worry and discontent? What would it look like to live with a little less worry and a lot more joy?

Philippians 4 contains the antidote to the ultimate Joy Taker with the definitive Joy Maker. This week you will learn practical steps to take to focus your mind and cast your cares on Christ.

Week Five

Day 1

"Trouble and anguish have come upon me,
yet Your commandments are my delight."
Psalm 119:143

*I*t almost sounds like Paul could have written this verse from Psalm 119, doesn't it? Ask God to help you delight in His word, despite trouble, anguish, or other circumstances.

Today your assignment will sound familiar. It's time to read and study Chapter 4 of Philippians. Before you begin, I would like for you to go back and read the entire book of Philippians again. As you read it, does it seem different now than a month ago? What concepts or topics do you see now that you didn't before you began your study?

What concepts or topics do you understand more fully now that you have studied this epistle?

With the context of the entire book in your mind, read and mark (if you are choosing to do so) Philippians 4. The following words or phrases are probably becoming very familiar to you:

Philippians
Christ Jesus
mind/attitude
rejoice
gospel

Do you see any possible Joy Takers in this chapter?

Philippians 4 begins with the word "therefore". This means there is a connection between the end of chapter 3 and the first few verses of chapter. Remember chapter divisions and verses were added to the Bible in later years, and this being a letter that was hand delivered, it would have been read in its entirety and in context.

Backing up a few verses, read Philippians 3:17 – 4:3 and answer the following questions:

What group of people does Paul describe in 3:18-19?

How are they identified? Hint: make a list from verse 19.

What contrast to this group do you see in verse 20?

Can you determine from these verses what the "therefore" in Philippians 4:1 is "there for"?

Record any other reflections or thoughts you have on Philippians 4.

Week Five

Day 2

"You are near, O Lord, and all Your commandments are truth."
Psalm 119:151

*A*re you aware of the Lord's nearness to you? Ask Him now to use His truth to set you free from any bondage that worry or doubt may have on you.

It almost seems unnecessary to begin this lesson by defining "worry." We surely all know what worry is, and some of you could be labeled as professional worriers. Those of us, who don't worry as much, probably worry those of you who do!

As a noun, the term "worry" means "a state of anxiety or uncertainty over actual or potential problems." However, as a verb, the word "worry" can be translated by a rather vivid visual: "to harass by tearing, biting, or snapping – especially at the throat." If you are a worrier, can you relate to this sensation? Can you feel your throat start to constrict as panic begins to set in over a set of circumstances you feel is out of control? Worry could be defined as the ultimate Joy Taker!

Much like the instruction given in Philippians 2 regarding grumbling and complaining, Paul was rather cut-and-dried on the subject of worry. Write out what you learn from Philippians 4:6-7 about worry. Be very specific – make a list or rewrite these verses in your own words. It might be helpful to look them up in different translations of the Bible. Because context is critical in Bible study, look back at Philippians 4:5. Write out the last four words of that verse and connect it to the first four verses of Philippians 4:6. What do you see?

Does the Bible have anything else to say about worry? Of course it does! The very best way to attack an enemy like worry is to build an arsenal, made up of God's Word, against it. Look up the following verses and write out what you learn about worry from each passage. For example, Psalm 55:22 says:

> "Cast your burden upon the Lord and He will sustain you;
> He will never allow the righteous to be shaken."

So you might say:
"When I begin to worry about <u>my finances</u>, I will <u>cast my concern about money upon God</u>. I won't let it shake me."

Isaiah 26:3

Isaiah 41:10 (see if you can find seven promises in the verse.)

Isaiah 43:1-2

Matthew 6:24-34

I Peter 5:6-7 (Do you see any prerequisite for casting your anxieties on the Lord?)

At the risk of this lesson becoming overly long, I want to ask you to read and study one more passage and answer some questions before you make your final summation about worry and how it relates to the believer.

Read 2 Chronicles 20 and list the chain of events as they occur.

Think through Jehoshaphat's prayer. Write out how he began his prayer.

How did Jehoshaphat petition God?

Compare 2 Chronicles 20 with Philippians 4:6. Any insights?

When did the Lord begin to rout out the enemy? Can you make a personal application here?

Write out 2 Chronicles 20:15. What does this verse mean to you right now in your present circumstances?

"Excuse me, your thoughts are showing"

Fifty thousand! According to neuroscientists that is the number of thoughts that the average person thinks daily. That is either good news or bad news, depending upon what we are thinking, because inevitably our thoughts convert into the words we speak and the things we do.

Matthew 12:34 tells us that "the mouth speaks out of what fills the heart." Most of us would just die if our every thought were posted on some jumbo screen for all to see. However, everyone can see our thoughts because they do translate into speech and action. Given that fact, we must be very thoughtful about our thinking, especially as we desire to live lives of true joy.

I learned this lesson the hard way. In a former university administrative position, I often gave status reports to a board of directors, men and women I wanted to impress. Once, in response to a board member's probing question, I answered, "May I be negative?" I meant to say, "May I be honest?" but I had been dwelling on the negative so long that it just inappropriately poured out of my mouth. I was embarrassed that I had put a negative foot forward and a board member could have rightly said, "Excuse me, Sheryl, but your negative thoughts are showing."

Paul, the author of Philippians, or the "epistle of joy", knew that thoughts were very important to living a life of true joy and he himself modeled solid mental discipline in this area. His positive thoughts showed up in the words he penned to the saints at Philippi encouraging them to rejoice and be joyful. Paul, himself, was filled with joyful gratitude each time he remembered the saints at Philippi (Philippians 1:3) and then he even affirmed how right he was to think confidently about their growth in Christ because he had them in his heart (mind):

"For it is only right for me to feel this way about you all, because I have you in my heart, since both in my imprisonment and in the defense and confirmation of the gospel, you all are partakers of grace with me." (Philippians 1:7)

Despite his imprisoned circumstances, Paul was able to rejoice in them and view them as "the greater progress of the gospel" and the cause for Christ becoming more well-known (Philippians 1:12-13). Paul's imprisonment didn't lock up his joyful thoughts towards the Philippians he held so dearly in his heart (mind) or about the cause of Christ for which he lived.

Billy Graham once wrote: "The happiness which brings enduring worth to life is not the superficial happiness that is dependent on circumstances. It is the happiness and contentment that fills the soul even in the most distressing circumstances and the most bitter environment. It is the kind of happiness that grins when things go wrong and smiles through the tears. The happiness for which our souls ache is one undisturbed by success or failure, one which will root deeply inside us and give inward relaxation, peace and contentment, no matter what the surface problems may be. That kind of happiness stands in need of no outward stimulus."

Most of us try to change and renew our circumstances (make more money, lose weight, improve relationships) when we should be asking God to renew our minds and thinking. When our minds are renewed, circumstances will take care of themselves and we might not mind if our thoughts are showing. (Sheryl)

Week Five

Day 3

"Many are my persecutors and my adversaries,
yet I do not turn aside from Your testimonies."
Psalm 119:157

Although we may not have very many physical persecutors, our thoughts can surely be our adversaries. Undisciplined thinking is a huge Joy Taker! This type of thinking can quickly lead to activities and conduct that could bring devastating consequences. It all starts with a single thought. In Philippians 4, we find two verses, which if we truly put into action, can revolutionize our thinking and behavior.

Read Philippians 4:8-9 and write out what these verses might "look like" in your own life. Don't miss the promise listed in verse 9.

How does the command in Philippians 4:8 relate to Philippians 4:6-7?

Often Scripture uses the words mind and heart interchangeably. Look up the following verses and add your thoughts and insights. Remember to personalize your statements – it will help cement these truths in your mind and heart!

Proverbs 4:23

Matthew 12:34

Romans 8:5-7

2 Corinthians 10:3-5 provides further insight into how we should evaluate our thoughts. Write out how this passage supports what you learned from the other verses relating to the mind and heart.

Now for the practical application – if you were to let Philippians 4:8 be your guide, how would it change the following things in your life? Be honest.

Reading

TV

Movies

Conversation

Thought Life

Social life

Companions

Do you think one of the reasons Paul could say in Philippians 4:11, "I have learned to be content in whatever circumstances..." is because he knew how to guard his mind?

It's not enough to monitor what goes in, we also have to establish in our minds what we believe about God. The foundation for contentment is resting in the Sovereignty of God. So as you end today's lesson on the heart and mind, look up the following passages and take time to meditate on who God is and what He is saying to you.

Deuteronomy 32:39

1 Chronicles 29:11-13

Daniel 4:35-37

Acts 17:24-25

Romans 8:28-29 (Even if these verses are familiar to you, read them in light of everything you've learned about Joy Takers and Joy Makers from the book of Philippians.)

Summarize your thoughts about how to guard your mind and heart, and why it is critical to your Christian walk.

Week Five

Day 4

"I rejoice at your Word, as one who finds great spoil."
Psalm 119:162

As our time with Paul and the Philippians draws to a close, do you find yourself rejoicing over the Word of God? Can you echo the psalmist and say you rejoice like one finding great spoil? Regardless of what's in our bank accounts, we are rich beyond measure when we consider our worth in Christ because of what He has done on our behalf.

What if you do have riches? Or what if you don't? What if you find yourself in need? What if you have the means to help others?

The last few verses of Philippians that we will study will cover the topic of giving and receiving. Can you think of any ways these two concepts can be Joy Takers or Joy Makers?

Read Philippians 4:14-19 and write out any insights you have about these verses.

With those verses in mind, carefully study the following two passages and list the principles regarding how and when to give.

2 Corinthians 8:1-15

2 Corinthians 9:6-15

Who sets the example for giving? See 2 Corinthians 8:9.

What do you learn about giving from 2 Corinthians 9:15?

Look up the following verses and write out any promises or commands related to giving. Is it always about money?

Psalm 41:1

Proverbs 25:21-22

1 John 3:17-18

"Who are you and what do you do?"

It's a very common scenario and takes place thousands of times every day all over the world. Two people meet for the first time and they engage in the "get to know each other" routine. Within minutes, this question will be asked, "What do you do?" Typically the answer to that question will be some sort of definition of a job or a place of employment. Sometimes how the person is dressed will give a clue to his or her occupation. If you were to ask Sheryl, "What do you do?" she would tell you, "I teach teachers." It's a rather simple explanation for the specific and unique call on her life and it explains a lot about who she is.

The apostle Paul, who had a rather impressive resume (he was a Pharisee among Pharisees! See Philippians 3:17.), identified himself rather simply in the first verse of Philippians. He called himself a bondservant. Now, in today's culture that is a foreign term, but in Bible times, everyone would have known exactly what he meant. A bondservant was a person who could be free, but chose to stay and serve his master and the master's family. For Paul to associate himself with this class of people made a huge statement. He was saying, "I could be a distinguished, leader but instead I am here to serve."

I think Paul sets an example for us in the way he humbly views himself because thinking more highly of ourselves than we should is a major Joy Taker in our lives.

Moving to the Northeast from Mississippi was not quite as traumatic as moving to another country where I would have had to learn a new language. Even so, I quickly realized there are catchphrases and sayings I used that just didn't translate here. Once I was talking with a friend who has a daughter the same age as mine. We were discussing how as children approach a certain age, a certain "attitude" tends to grow along with them. My friend said, "Yep! My girl's gotten on her furry britches."

I had no idea what she meant so I asked her to repeat it. When she did, I heard the same catchphrase "furry britches". Being new to the Northeast, I assumed it had something to do with the cold weather and maybe her daughter had fur-lined pants. Just to verify, I asked one more time and she said, "In the South, you don't say someone gets too big for their britches?" Oh! Not "furry britches", but too big **for her** britches. In other words, her daughter was too full of herself and it showed in her attitude.

Thinking too highly of ourselves will steal our joy every single time. A very good indicator of crossing this line is when we spend more time thinking about our rights than we do our privileges. We think about what we are owed rather than what we can freely offer to others. We put our schedules, wants, needs and desires at the top of the "to-do" list and expect everyone else to take our list and make it their priority. Then we wonder what happened to our joy.

What a contrast to Paul's attitude! What a greater contrast to the attitude of Jesus who, before He was crucified for our sins, took on the lowliest role of all and washed the feet of His disciples (John 13:1-17). That might be stunning enough, but to think He willingly washed the feet of someone ready to betray Him goes beyond our human belief. He set the supreme example: **"If I then, the Lord and the Teacher, washed your feet, you also ought to wash one another's feet" (John 13:14).**

Jesus, Who was the radiance of God's glory and the exact representation of God's nature and Who upholds all things by the word of His power, took on the role of a servant. That thought should fill us all with awe and wonder.

It's hard to wash feet while wearing furry britches. Maybe it's time we check how we identify ourselves by what we are wearing. (Cammy)

CPSIA information can be obtained at www.ICGtesting.com
Printed in the USA
BVOW061115100313

315158BV00002B/5/P